All Author Royalties wil_ _ _ _ _ _

Hospiscare

To Lyn & Keith,

I hope you enjoy this Little Book of Poetry between Judith (94 years old) and myself.

    All Best wishes,

      John.

A Selection of Poems

How it all started…

This is a record and result of three years of communications between a Residential manager, (myself) and a resident, Judith Putt at an independent retirement community, "Raleigh Court" (pronounced "Ral-lay") in the South of England.

One day in 2005, not long after I had arrived, Mrs Putt dropped a note - that was to become a series of notes through the manager's letterbox.

It was a Monday morning and I had just returned from my holiday in Cornwall. I picked up a deluge of mail and flicked through the usual pile of unwanted bills and then came across an unusual handwritten letter.

Naturally, I opened this first. Curiously, it was written in rhyme from start to finish. I proceeded to read the delightful verse and it immediately brought a smile to my face.

After finishing that very first rhyme, I knocked upon her door in order to thank her for this creative and uplifting note. Of course, (as I was to find out) Mrs Putt was out for the day as she was most every day. Then again, the next day, I went along to her apartment and tapped upon the door - with exactly the same result; she was out again. I scratched my head - both mentally and physically. What to do?

I decided to set about answering her note, and realized that at the very least it merited a reply in rhyme (something I had never seriously attempted since childhood).

After numerous attempts (and my brain straining for catchy rhymes), scrunched up balls of paper were soon laying all about my feet, I finally and gingerly placed my completed rhyme back through her letterbox.

It seemed like I had hardly blinked when I found yet another rhyme on the office doormat. Here was another reply to my own recent and rather laboured effort. (And I still hadn't seen the resident since my return from holiday). With the new rhyme in hand; here I was, under pressure to reply in rhyme again!

On top of that, hadn't my last poem taken an age to construct! Anyway, reply I did, and our communication continued in this fashion for the next three years laced with much banter and teasing that went back and forth ... with an added competitive edge as to who could write a rhyme better and quicker, with tongues firmly in cheek ... and with irreverent tones... that was how the duel between the "Bard" and the "Brilliant Mind" all began.

After a substantial time had passed, I got to thinking about our rhyming correspondence. I pulled out all of the poems and letters from an old box I had haphazardly put them all in.

The scraps of paper lay across my desk filling up every

inch. There seemed to be hundreds of them! I put them into sequence (as best as I could recall and matching them up with my own responses) and set about typing them up on my computer. On a whim, I sent the poems along to my publisher.

So, here are the results - as written - of our communication and ultimately of our friendship, all created in rhyming verse... I hope you enjoy them.

John

The Poems

*J*ohn, John, where are you, John?
The patio wants sweeping,
And autumn leaves from all those trees,
Are in the entrance creeping.

All the boards are bare and blank,
No notice to be seen,
The refuse room requires a broom,
The bins are not too clean.

Now you know,
What we must bear -
Alone
Because our John's not there.

Judith
***

Behind the door, amongst a pile of bills
I found your rhyming letter...
Reading your sweet verse and lament
Made me feel so much better.

And thank you for asking about my holiday
We went to Cornwall on a tour
We ate, and walked and talked
And ate some more.

But rest assured
I hope you agree
We'll soon return
To something like normality.

I will sweep the leaves
Wash the bins, you will see
To restore
Raleigh to its former beauty.

But before I do these deeds
There's something to do, that's key
Two little words, to write,
"On Duty!"

John
***

*H*ow long did it take you?
To write that little rhyme?
I wouldn't mind surmising,
It took a long, long time!

In a flash I'll write a poem,
So therefore you will find,
Whatever else I haven't got,
I have a brilliant mind!

Judith
***

(Envelope addressed to 'Wordsworth, Longfellow and Scott')

Yes, I have to admit
Thinking on the spot like this
Leaves me rather short on wit.

It pains me to say
That I just have to concede
I've really lost my way.

I'm no Longfellow or Scott I know
That may be very true - but unlike your quick mind
This is the best that I can do!

John
***

*Please John, can you help me?
A remedy I seek
I have this very awkward door
That has a nasty squeak.*

*Nothing much upsets me
I've coped with many-a leak
But one thing I cannot do
Is stop that wretched squeak!*

Judith
***

Oh dear! What can I say?
About the squeak that won't go away.

When I left, it seemed okay
Alas, it seems it is here to stay.

Never fear though - you will see
The introduction of my "Plan B".

After that, and another day
I think that noise may well have gone away.

I know that irksome squeak is not so nice
But remember - *it could be worse* - it could be mice!

John
***

Regarding writing poems
I thought I was the queen
But now alas, I can't be sure
I have your efforts seen.

I might ignore you now - but wait
I've never been unkind
Whatever odd odes you compose
I keep my brilliant mind.

By the way, what makes you think
That rodents are not nice?
Nasty doors with nasty squeaks?
I'd rather have the mice!

Judith

I'm sending my thanks to you
For such kind praise
In the form of this poem
As opposed to more usual ways.

I'll await your instructions
To get back to work
And resolve that blessed squeak
You know I will not shirk.

If I don't see you today
And you do not pass my door
Happily, I will know -
That pesky squeak is no more!

John

*R*egretfully, I have to say
That @#*%* squeak is here to stay.
And yes I passed your office door
"At a meeting" - but what for?

Guess it's just a waste of time
Here I go - another rhyme.

Judith
***

*W*e did our best with all our might
An answer we did seek.
In spite of all our efforts
There's still that devilish squeak.

We tried and tried again
Our brains were much too weak.
Now I'm going to bed to dream
Of that confounded squeak.

Judith
***

I would have preferred
That you had not
Mentioned *that* word.

You know which one I mean,
It begins with an 'S' and ends in 'K'
It can be heard but remains unseen.

But in a day or two
I sometimes find
There's usually something else to do.

The thing to which I refer
Is something else to fix and repair
And that first thing is suddenly on "defer".

Some call it bad luck; some call it "Murphy's Law",
But when it does strike
I am sure you will forget that bloody door!

John

O kay, okay, I'm sure you're right
Another crisis will appear
I only hope if it does
The Poet Laureate won't be here.

No - because I hope to be -
At glorious Sidmouth by-the-Sea.

Judith

Off to Sidmouth - there's a treat
Oh, how the "other half" live,
To do that -
You don't know what I'd give.

The shops, the gardens
And the sea
It's a far cry
From your squeaking misery.

Did you eat buns and have Cream Tea?
Visit coffee shops galore?
Then, pat your tummy and say;
'Thank you - but no more.'

Did you take your bucket?
And your spade?
Along the sandy shoreline
A dig followed by a wade.

Oh,
What stories you will tell...
All the while I've been sitting here
In my tiny prison cell! (Office).

John
***

*O*ff I went to Sidmouth
A very pleasant ride
When I got there - what to do
I really must decide.

Yes, I walked the gardens
And along the windy shore
And had a coffee and two buns
And looked around for more.

Then came along a shower of rain
Which didn't bother me
I had another coffee
Which ended up to three.

Then the time was half past twelve
I wanted things to munch
Well - a girl can't write a poem
Without a bit of lunch.

I go on throughout my happy day
I gave a fleeting thought
To all the folk in prison cells
Especially Raleigh Court!

Judith
***

Thank you for your poem
        Glad you enjoyed your day
        The only problem now is
I don't know what to say.

I could talk about the weather
And what it's going to do
Or the latest gossip
But I know that's not for you.

I could write about this or that
Not very much at all
It's so quiet at Raleigh
I can watch and count the leaves that fall.

Will anything happen today?
That I can write in my ode
It may do later on
Perhaps I should put this on hold.

So I will finish where I started
With nothing much to say
No tidbits to offer, my parting comment,
'What a grey and dreary day!'

John
***

How can you say things are quiet?
What about the chatter?
Men and women all alike
Do nothing else but natter.

Do you sit there just to count
How many leaves are falling?
Can't you see the little birds
And hear the seagulls calling?

Depressing day? But never mind
Tomorrow will be better
You will have a new surge of life
Now you've read this letter!

(But warning!)

However much you rack your brains
The brilliant mind to sweeten
I'm a bit like Tesco's pies
I never will be beaten!

Judith
***

The brilliant rhyming mind is right
Who would know better?
You hit the nail on the head
In your recent letter.

But careful I must be
Or I fear your head will grow
With all this sudden praise
And it'll be me you'll not want to know.

The only question I have for you
Is regarding of not how, but why?
It concerns why you liken yourself
To a certain Tesco's Pie.

So, tell me about that pie…
Are you sure it's not soft on top - or fried to a crisp?
Or overcooked in the middle
And gone up in a wisp?

But alas, I must go now
I've finished my last "cuppa"
You brought light to a dark day
Thankfully, it's time for supper.

So ends another day
Our poems have all been heard
A brilliant mind? Unbeatable? Maybe so,
But at least I'll have the final word!

John

I've got this nasty feeling someone's
Out to steal my thunder
I may be wrong, but let me say
They've made a king-size blunder.

Must make a serious effort
To cut them down to size
For I'm the only one to say
I'm tops - like Tesco's pies!

Last word - have another thought
I am the brains of Raleigh Court!

Judith
***

You are a clever girl
With your rhyming pies and tea
We'll have to joust some more
And the result we will see.

Yes, you are very smart
And this thing they call "IQ"
You want me to believe
They designed it just for you.

Your prose is very good
I do enjoy your rhymes
And you seem to have the knack
Of writing the very best of lines.

But there's something I must say
And please do not pout
Regarding "someone's" brains at Raleigh Court
The jury is still out!

Have you heard the one
About the chicken and the eggs
Which one comes first
The question still begs...

If you answered that
I wonder what you'd say,
Throw in the validity of your mind
I'll answer that - if I may.

My best guess is this
With a huff and deep sigh
You'll say;
'Easy, that's Tesco's (frozen) chicken pie!'

John
***

Thank you for your kind remarks
And even grudging praise
Simple efforts are worthwhile
If a laugh they raise.

I'm very fond of chickens

If they're sitting in a nest
I wouldn't like one in a pie
Not even Tesco's best!

You specify a jury
What's behind my back?
I'd better try to find my gun
Be ready to attack.

I'm very calm and controlled
And not consumed with fury
Let us get just one thing straight
Who's acting as this jury?

When will the panel sit again
To clarify my lot?
Perhaps you think I'm worried
I assure you that I am not.

I'm confident that my IQ
Will hold me in good stead
Losing my standing as the best?
No - that can't be said.

P.S. Any sweeties do you wish
So you can fill your little dish?

Judith
*****

Alas, I cannot think of a word
That rhymes with pie
Hold on a moment
I'll give it one more try.

Judge and jury
I do not want to be
I've enough on my plate
I'm sure you will agree.

So I'll pass the buck
Over to you
I'm out of a pickle
You'll be in a stew.

What was that about a gun?
Did I hear you right?
If so - you can be sure
I will be extra polite.

Now that you have become
Raleigh's judge and jury
I can't help wondering
What you will decree?

But wait - I think I know
From this faux court
You will bestow
Your great wisdom and thought.

And from this high power

How will you address the rest?
'Look at me,' you'll say,
'I am the best!'

John
***

You can wring your hands
And grind your teeth and even tear your hair
The brutal truth remains the same
It's known everywhere.

And if you don't believe me
I'll put your mind to rest
In all this known world of ours
I know that I'm the best.

What???

You cannot think what rhymes with pie?
Does it make you want to cry?
Then you stop and wonder why
You'll never be a clever guy
Thet's yer lot - the end is nigh

Your last attempt is most revealing
Someone near, my fame is stealing
Which of course is quite a threat
On your guard - it will be met.

Once I had to serve as jury
I'm no hand at give and take
I'd no mercy - sure he's guilty!
Now you know the judge I'd make!

Judith
***

I presently find myself
Thinking of words that rhyme
In fact,
I seem to be doing it all of the time.

I hope it's not serious
I don't know what to do
Lately, it's become compulsive
What about for you?

And during the day
I try to think of something witty
To go back
And write in my little ditty.

The bank manager told me
What I'd written under, 'Nat West'
It's quite embarrassing really,
He told me I'd written; 'not the best.'

So I went to see the doctor
Do you know what he said?
Take two days off -
And get home to bed.

So if you notice
When we talk next time
I keep muttering repeatedly
I'm simply trying to find the perfect rhyme.

So here I go again
With these words rattling around my head
And still wondering
What's been left unsaid?

And I have to confess
I've exaggerated just a bit
That part about the doctor
No two days off, just; 'not to rhyme and sit.'

So I get up and about
And when I feel the urge coming on
He gave me a simple remedy -
Go ahead, and burst out into song!

John
***

I assume from your ramblings
That time after time
You're trying all day
To make something rhyme.

I wish I could help you
But method I lack
You see I'm afraid
That you haven't the knack.

You actually need brains
(Assuming they're there)
But don't start a song
That wouldn't be fair!

The whole thing has you in its grip
You'll have to cut it out
Or we'll have singing all day long
Of that I have no doubt.

Sarcasm as the poets wrote
Is the lowest form of wit
Very useful if you wish
To get a counter-hit!

My rhyming's not compulsive
I expect by now you've guessed
I have the brains with which to cope
Because I am the best!

Judith

I'm sorry to disappoint you
I know it must be hard
When you haven't heard
From your favourite Bard.

After a while
In next to no time
I will return
With a brand new rhyme.

This week has gone so fast
I wonder where it went
The trials of Raleigh
Have left me totally spent.

Although I can't resist
Adding another verse
This poem I sincerely hope
Won't get any worse.

Because I think you secretly long
To hear a tune to you from me,
Here goes;
A lovely melody.

"Your heads in the clouds
High up in the sky
Thinking about the fact
You are the best pie!"

Okay, the dogs may bark

And the cats may wail
On hearing my voice
Nowhere in sight a wagging tail.

So, what do you think?
Of my little jingle
Do you think
It will make a hit single?

So that's all for now
I've enjoyed our banter and cheek
My creative pen is done
I'll be back in a week.

I'll get back to you
When I've a suitable word
One that rhymes with brain
Excuse my French - but 'oh, *Merde!*'

John
***

I can say what rhymes with, 'Brains'
It's what your poems cause
'Pains' - they're here and everywhere
Never seem to pause.

Because you keep concocting
That mind-disturbing verse
To one who really can write poems
There's surely nothing worse.

But there - you do your very best
No one can do more
And who am I to mark your work
Pretending I'm the law.

If you started singing
The cats would start to sneeze
The dogs would bark and I myself
Would not be very pleased!

And if you sang to your dog
I think you'd hear her wail
Because you carry her
She couldn't even wag her tail!

But I digress - I have to thank you
For your lengthy letter
Now if you'll forgive me
I'll try for something better.

Now we get to other things

How good was your weekend?
We didn't go to Salcombe
They have a room to mend.

And round and round and round you go
To get right to the end
But by the time you do get there
You're really round the bend!

But Exmouth was a happy choice
I'm glad that we were wise
And good old 'Woolies' didn't fail
T'was there I brought this prize.

I'm contrite now and sorry
That I ridiculed your work
I hope you see your way
To take this well-intentioned perk.

Now I hie me to my bed
Why sleep? I'm sure you've guessed
I need to top up energy
Because - You know the rest!

Judith
*****

P hew! I'm glad you weren't my teacher
There's no telling what you'd do,
With a red pen in your hand
And all the words you'd strike it through.

But I think you'd be quite fair
With your students reciting Shelly and Keats
And reward the very best ones
With lashings of *Quality Streets.*

This poem is brief I know
It's not that I can't find a rhyme
It's just at the moment
I really don't have the time.

I've a Guest room to change
A vacuum to mend
And when you see me next
I'll be either up the wall or round the bend.

Alas, though something else is amiss
My chance to enjoy a thrill
It's those *Rocher* chocolates you gave me
They're in my desk drawer untouched still...

John
***

You say your poems very short
You cannot find a rhyme
Leave the Guest room and the vac.
And then you'd have the time.

But then I'm sure if duty calls
You'll be there on the spot
But simmer down a little bit
The pace seems very hot.

As for climbing up the wall
One thing comes to mind -
You'd be up top and that would mean
We'd all be left behind.

But there's another meaning
To that phrase if I recall,
And someone has to rescue you
And ease you down that wall.

One thing I would like to do
Make things very clear
I'm not a Brownie or a Guide
And not a volunteer!

But perhaps by now you've simmered down
Let sanity prevail!
If not - tuck into choccies
Sweeties never fail!

I hope you're feeling better now

And had a little rest
I'm okay and you know why?
Because I am still the best!

Judith
***

*M*y little clock sits on the oven
Keeping time just so,
But nothing lasts forever
And now the damn thing's slow.

Or will be in a day or two
Hence this little rhyme
Could you be so kind and make it,
Show the proper time?

Judith
***

I'd like to have seen your face
Before you'd recovered from the shock
Of having got up so early
And not having adjusted that old clock.

It won't be dark outside
Now you're back on "GMT"
When you look outside out the window
You should be able to see.

By the way - watch how you go
Writing poems on public trans-port
You could miss your stop
And there goes Raleigh Court.

So if I don't hear from you
And sometime our acquaintance we shall renew
I'll know you've been writing poems on buses
And ended up in Timbuktu!

John
***

Indeed I rose at 5 o' clock
But wits are none the worse
In fact, they've turned out pretty well
Behold a 3 minute verse.

I had a cup of coffee
To start this bit of fun

I hadn't finished drinking when
See the verse is done!

You surely cannot write a poem
So quickly - that is clear
I think that it would take you
At least another year!

As for writing on the bus
I won't miss any stops
I'll be on full alert because
My clock is now the tops.

Shall I miss the stop one day?
See the journey through?
No - I have a horrid thought
I don't like Timbuktu!

Therefore I'll not wander
Until my poems are done
I'll luxuriate in situ
All snug at 21!

But now - whatever you may do
Go east or wander west
You won't beat my 3 minute verse
Because I am the best!

Judith
***

What took you so long?
I'll beat that by a minute
Takes me down to two
I'd better be quick and begin it.

Twilight dreams and thoughts
Will all be here to read
Please come together
So I can complete this two minute deed.

I just had a vision
Of you sitting snug in 21
Trying to write a poem
And barely having begun.

The night is drawing in
It's dark out not light
There you are at your bureau
Still there trying to write.

Now its half past ten
Most have gone to bed
But Judith is still there sitting
With words flailing about her head.

The hedgehogs are coming out
The badgers are on the run
All's quiet at Raleigh,
Except the scrunching sound of paper from 21.

The postman's already here

The morning papers on the mat
That now uncomfortable chair
Is where Judith is still sat.

It is finally completed
She'll get some fitful rest,
And she'll come by tomorrow
Still claiming she's the best.

I still have time to say sorry though
For my teasing and my cheek
Because if I'm really honest
I thought that poem would take another week!

John
***

*R*eading through your poem
I think you had a dream
Taking day's to write a verse?
Using paper by the ream?

In your airy-fairy vision
Were you visualizing me?
I, who am the very best,
You know that's clear to see.

And as for your assertion
That you wrote in double time
I challenge you to prove that
By writing one more rhyme.

Occasionally I worry
That one day you'll compose
A real mind-shattering poem
Instead of third-rate prose.

But if I lost my favourite place
I'd put things to the test
And prove that now and for all time
I am the very best! (I think).

And don't look so blue
You know that it's true
More to come, Monday
If I have time Sunday.

Judith

Hello, it's me again
Please don't frown or sigh
Here's my riposte to your challenge
A quick (and sparkling) reply!

It was no dream I had
I was reading between the lines
With your on-going struggle
Of finding suitable rhymes.

And there was me - writing so quickly
At my desk with drinking cup
Creating verse after verse
With still more coffee left to sup.

And before that - at breakfast table
Over a nice hot muffin,
I reeled off another verse
But please! Praise me not, it was really nothing!

So how long has elapsed
I'm not sure when I started this,
But I am sure that you'll tell me
If it's a hit or if it's a miss.

What was that you said?
I'm in the third division?
I'll have to get promoted
And work on my revision.

I'll soon be up there with you

In the Premier league
But if it means staying up all night
I'm sure I'll suffer from fatigue.

So, my humble apologies
There was I, in the belief
That you writing all those poems
Was like pulling aching teeth!

Here I was thinking...
You were working all night
Sharing waking time with the owls
By the burning candle light.

So, I'll believe you
If you say it really isn't true
Upset the brilliant mind?
That's something I wouldn't want to do!

John
***

I've had to go to Salcombe
Lest my temper should get worse
I can't believe you thought I took
So long to write a verse.

Such cruel accusations!
I was almost in despair
But Salcombe now has calmed me down

I'll leave my temper there.

Now I'm back at Raleigh Court
I've had a change of mind
I'm sure you didn't mean to be
Uncharacteristically unkind.

But now I've read your latest verse
My tempers back and much, much worse!

How come we're into football?
It surely is agreed,
Compared with writing poetry
It's in a different league.

But I'm sure you'll stay in third
That is my decision
Unless perchance there just might be
A 21st Division.

But it seems you have regrets
I'm sure you will find
You will not write a verse which could
Upset my brilliant mind!

P.S. Just in case you're short of treats
Here are all the usual sweets
But mark all through your busy day
My temper hasn't gone away. (Well, not quite).   *Judith*

Is it safe to come out now?
You sounded in quite a rage,
I've kept my head low
But I know the reason - I'll wage.

It was the last poem that did it
But it was meant to be a tease
So I'll put my thinking cap on
And try to appease.

Or should I put my helmet on?
As if I'm at war
And put barricades up
Right outside my office door.

But to let you know
I've given you the benefit of doubt
So the next time I see you
You'll be less likely to shout.

And if you suddenly cross the road
When you next see me
This apology hasn't worked
How about an invite to tea?

I'm glad you enjoyed Salcombe
And left your temper there
Seeing you mad and grumpy
Is something I couldn't bear.

If you are mad tomorrow

When I test those alarm bells
You could go always go back to Salcombe
To de-stress and collect sea shells.

But I don't think you'll stay mad
At least not for long
Even if you do believe
It was me that was wrong.

To soothe you a bit
It must have been in my dreams
You working all night long
Is a question now it seems.

Hang on! What's this?
There's "choccies" hanging on my door,
Happily this grovelling apology
May not be needed anymore!

John
***

*P*ut your helmet in the bin
For now I've changed my ways
   Gosh - what am I saying?
I must be in a haze.

I cannot change my ways too much
It's more than you deserve
I'll keep some ammunition
As a sensible reserve.

You ask if there is any job
To ease your guilty mind?
Yes - write a decent verse
Say, Poet Laureate kind.

But that is wishful thinking
I'm forever doomed to see
Dreadful verse that comes my way
Oh well - bad luck for me

However I'm resilient
Nothing gets me down
I'd pack my bag and wander off
To lovely Salcombe town.

Now it's time to stop this lark
And no I'm not obsessed
But really I must emphasize
I am the very best!

                                        Judith

I think the war is over
But should I lapse or even jest
I'm stating categorically
I think you are the best.

Okay, now that's over
I can have a little fun
Teasing you just a little
I've only just begun.

You want prose of quality
Didn't you receive my lovely verse?
What was your verdict?
Between average and much worse...

You see - I was only trying to match
The standard of your own pen
And when you do up your game
Please let me know when.

I'm not talking of football
Although it's a good analogy
The score is one-all
Let's see if you can beat me.

But your defence is slow, your attack mundane
The ball deflects in play
You just scored an own goal
And made it my winning day!

So the moral of the tale;

3rd Division teams can sometimes beat or whip
The high flying Premier teams
That lack witty zip!

John
***

*Y*our subtle innuendo
      Has fallen on deaf ears
      I'm pretty sure your aim
Was getting me in tears.

(Note this little poem)

'Should they whisper false of you
Do not trouble to deny
Should the words they say be true?
Storm and weep and swear they lie.'

What's this - you really mean it?
No kidding - not a jest?
In your opinion it seems that
I am … you know the rest.

What can I say? Those adverse words
I wrote - I still recall
One more moment you will find
The tears will start to fall.

Hang on - what's this I see
I played a lousy game?

Now my tempers coming back
No one damn's my name.

Especially when they intimate
That lowly third could win
Never while I'm in the team
Take that on the chin.

You have come perilously near
To rocking me up high
But top me, you never will do
However much you try.

Your poem started off so well
I actually felt benign
But sadly now I have to say
It's suffered a decline.

As I said - do your best
With very little brain
And the little bit you do have
Is sadly on the wane.

But now you've read my little verse
And all that's off my chest
I'm very pleased you admit
I am the very best!

Judith
***

Yes, it's true,
I can't philosophize with Plato
Write like Jane Austen
Or head up an organization such as NATO.

But I can still joust with you
And I have a good brain
After reading this - you'll agree
It's hardly on the wane.

As I've said this before;
I aim to be on a par
With the standard I meet
Whether a mini-cooper or Ferrari racing car.

'Oh no!' I hear you say,
'Not another analogy!'
But I think it's mighty useful
If it helps you to see.

Imagine if you're racing me in a car
And I see you in my rear-view mirror,
I'll go down through the gears
And allow you to get a little nearer.

And in the unlikely event
You should edge ahead of me
I'll put my foot on the gas
And I'm right there for you to see.

So now we've established

I'm a good race track driver
Roaring along
Able to see inside your windscreen visor.

And sometimes I'll let you go in front
To make you feel good
But not in sympathy
I hope that's understood.

No, what I mean to say;
That it's a dangerous thing
If a racing car driver should cry
You could crash or have a bad ding.

Please take lightly what I say,
So please no more tears
It would really help me to
Alleviate my fears.

And when I take my foot off the pedal
It's not to give this old car a rest
It's to let you go on past – shouting,
'Look I'm winning! I am the best!'

John
***

I am a maiden Fair you know
   I'm not a man at all
   I do not toy with racing cars
Or kick a silly ball.

So please take special note of this,
I'm of the Fairer sex
I hope I've made that very clear
It's best to clear the decks.

Now for the nitty-gritty
You say you have a brain
I bet you had a little bath
And washed it down the drain.

As folk that chase about in cars
Along a busy road
Never mind who gets in front
They break the HighwayCode.

That I fear is worrying me
What if 'they' caught our John
(He who think he writes a poem
As good as maestro Donne).

So please take special care
When trying to win the race
Acknowledge that I am tops
And that's my proper place.

I'm busy but I'm clever
Some other folk are not
It's a question of ability
And what brain power you've got.

You see I do what you can't do
Something being deficient
I do four jobs all at once
Brain-power being sufficient!

And all the jobs are properly done
No skipping bits and pieces
No ironing clothes and leaving them
With scorch marks and creases.

Now the final episode;

I emphasize with zest
It must be clear to you by now
I AM THE VERY BEST!

Judith
***

You've probably wondered
Where the Bard has been?
No notes through your door
And hardly has he been seen.

I'm sure you've missed my thoughts
And my philosophy
So I'll knock out a quick verse
As I drink my Earl Grey Tea.

I do enjoy your odes
They sometimes make me laugh and roar
Over some particular claims
I have to pick myself up off the floor!

You do like to tell tall tales
And oft make an extraordinary claim
I'll assume they're all tongue in cheek
If it's all the same

'The very best at this,'
'The very best at that,'

When I read of all of this
Not an eyelid will I bat.

So I'll nod in agreement
And as a matter of fact
I'll do something else -
I'll use old-fashioned tact.

But I've had my bit of fun
I hope you're not mad in a twirl
Because I really do think
You are a very clever girl.

And all joking aside
When your poems lilt, dance and rhyme
They sometimes can be
Really quite sublime.

And If I twisted your arm
I think you secretly delight
In my poetry-like musings
That I specifically write.

Alas, the tea leaves I see
I'll have to end this now
Why don't you give a curtsy
And I'll take a bow.

John
***

*N*ow I really am bereft
No post for many a day
When the Bard will write again
It's difficult to say.

Has the old brain failed again?
No matter - I'm sure
It will liven up a bit
And you'll write verse(?) once more.

But wait oh joy - what's this I see,
Something on the floor
Someone must have climbed the stairs
And shoved it through my door.

I hesitate to open it
Let the pleasure last
As if I'm not mistaken
I'll need the brandy fast!

Now I've had a good old swig
I've dared to read your verse
After all I've read the lot
This one's not much worse.

Now I know the problem
It's very plain to see
You cannot write a proper verse
On cups of Earl Grey Tea.

Sparkling verse - fantastic poems?

You sure can kid yourself
Put you to a proper test
You'd soon be on the shelf.

And far from banishing my woes
I'm sorry to affirm
That when I read your 'sparkling verse'
They all came back Full-Term.

I do however seem to sense
A little air of praise
For all my efforts poetry-wise
So I must change my ways.

I now confirm that all your rhymes
Are worthy of your name
(Maybe they're a little odd)
Delightful all the same.

I've read a verse
My tempers worse.

Tongue in cheek! What do you mean?
I hope it's said in jest
You just will not admit
That I am undeniably the best!

Judith
***

Do I detect a hint of praise?
If I do - you're quite astute
Thinking my sparkling poems
Are really rather cute.

But then - my second thought
That brandy you sip
Is the real reason
For the ceasing of you letting rip.

But insulted I am not
Should it be brandy you need
For my offerings to become
Sparkling indeed.

But before you gloat
I should add here a word or two
I also have a pain-reliever
Known as a special brew.

'What's that?' I hear you ask
It's not to be feared
Each time I've read a verse of yours,
Another shot of whiskies disappeared!

So when you see me about
With my hands held to my head
I've been reading your latest
And with a headache gone to bed.

Ha! So now the truth is all out!

I write my verse whilst drinking tea
You confront mine with a brandy chug
And I - yours, with a pitcher of whisky!

John
***

Now I know how to write a verse
Sadly you need a drink
To make this latest offering
How many did you sink?

Please be careful and refrain
From sipping too much booze
Think of all your little dears
And how much you could lose.

I'm getting very worried
It's all too much for you
You'll end up an alcoholic
And then what will we do.

So come right off the bottle
Stick to Earl Grey Tea
Then a stunning poem
Might evolve for me to see.

That's wishful thinking I'm afraid
I'll never have that pleasure

When I think of what could be
I need another measure!

You say you get a headache
I don't know what you mean
Because although you have two ears
There's little in between!

So all your rude remarks
Are treated with disdain
Well - perhaps I am a little harsh
I don't like causing pain.

So here is just one word of praise
Sometimes you get it right
Even if it takes a while
Probably all night!

All the same I must repeat
That I am truly blessed
Because I am the only one
Who is the very best! (So there!)

Be kind or the judge
Will give you hard labour
Cursed is he
Who smiteth his neighbour!!

Judith
***

P lease pass this along;
     To the Raleigh Egghead
          The one who says she's so smart
Are we to assume she's also well-read?

'The Bard, (she says);
Has cotton wool stuffed between his ears'
Due to the "fact"
He's drank one too many beers.

But that was just poetic licence that I used
That I should need a drink
To finish reading her verse
What did she think?

A tonic is nice - but in moderation
I'm happy more often than not
- *I hope you'll believe me* -
To simply drink tea by the pot.

The grey cells are diminishing
Or so she'll imply,
But I'm here to contest my mental capacity
With truth! Honesty! And no lie!

Her mantra-like claim goes,
'I'm such a clever clogs,'
'And your brain', she will say;
'Has already gone to the dogs.'

But I have my full quota

Of those tiny grey cells
And don't mock surprise now as if
You've just heard those alarm bells.

I'm able to rationalize and intellectualize
This loaf's not dull but bright,
Unlike talking heads that over-theorize
It's always switched on and light.

Nothing fuzzy going on here
I've my wits about me
With lots of common sense to spare
I'll have to help you to see.

And if you want some help
With any problem you know who to ask
Because you should know by now
I'm easily able to multi-task.

I'll try to illuminate you
Although it's not startling information
But I'm sad to say
For you it seems like a revelation.

So when you get home
Be careful which button you press
One is on and the other is off,
Get it wrong and you'll be in a right mess.

And before you get the wrong end
Of the proverbial stick

There is no electrician needed for this
It should be what makes you tick.

And when I see you again
There will be no need to impress
That my bright intellect is high
You won't be able to say anything less.

To recap; if it's still muddy and dark
My light is on all seven days of the week
Remember to flick your switch
And you'll have the answer you seek.

But if you should find yourself feeling dull
You may have hit the wrong switch
Take stock of your flat
Your Christmas lights may be on full-pitch!

John
***

*I*t seems you have a nasty cough
I'm sorry for your plight
  You shouldn't try your little brain
That dreadful "verse" to write.

That is sure to get you down
Oh hell - you've tried again
Why is it my bad luck that you
Must inflict such pain.

And I see you've gone against
All we have to do
Wasting paper by the quire
And writing rubbish too!

And do you really think that you
Are Raleigh's shining light?
Never a little flicker
By day or even night?

You say your grey cells are okay
And working to the dot
One day I'll put you to the test
And prove they are not!

Throughout your run-down "poetry"
Correct me if I'm wrong
I think you're trying to needle me
But my resolve is strong.

To prove it all just note the verse

I've written at the end
Read-mark - and inwardly digest
These words to you I send.

And cups of tea are for the weak
Like members of the lounge
If I ever should chance within
A nice liquor I'd scrounge.

Your intellect is high - your light is on
Who do you think you're kidding?
All I can see is just a void
And even that's with fiddling!

But worry not - enjoy your day
I've given up the fight
To try to get a decent verse
You'll never get it right!

Not like me - I must repeat
I emphasize it lest
You should ever doubt that I
Am quite the very best!

It matters not how straight the gate
How charged with punishment the scroll
I am the master of my fate
I am the captain of my soul.

Judith
***

I have a little request
Something for you to do;
Replace a few words here and there
From your latest review.

The words to which I refer
Concerns descriptions of my brain
Such as "void", "run-down",
And shockingly how my verse causes you "pain".

They can easily be replaced
It wouldn't take you long
And concerning my fine mind
You can see that they are wrong!

I can almost hear you saying,
'What's he going on about?'
It's very simple really
Let me help you out.

There's a host of words
Good ones to use
Rather than those other ones
Which are meant for abuse.

Let me tell you something
You see praise is the key
Added to that
Is a discerning use of vocabulary.

And while we're on the subject

When you change those words
Our relationship will be flying
Just like those migrating birds.

Might I suggest a few to you;
To describe my big head
How about, "sharp", "intuitive" and "smart"
Therefore creating poetry that's well-read.

So I'll trust you to revise
In your own good time
With these new words
P.S. You might even make it rhyme!

Note:
The Bard is off tomorrow
You'll have to wait to next week
To receive another work from him
And the reply to yours you seek.

John
***

*From your latest effort
I sense you miss the praise
That I should fairly give you
Right - I'll mend my ways.*

*I think perhaps I may have been
A little harsh with you*

I'll have to put the record straight
I'll see what I can do.

First of all I have to state
How lucky we are here
To have you looking after us
To know that you are near.

Have I really used such words?
As "void" (regarding brains),
I have to say I didn't mean
To cause you any pains.

You - who are the greatest poet,
The genius of all times
I wish that I could be like you
And write such witty rhymes.

Now are your ruffled feathers soothed
And harmony restored?
I trust your forlorn feelings
Have vanished by the board.

So if you feel I've made amends
For every damning thought
Try to have a good weekend
Away from Raleigh Court.

After that I hear you say
Are her fingers crossed?
Well - as to that I cannot say

Not at any cost!

I do however have a poem
That might make people wait
To read it through and then proceed
To carefully shut the gate!

And now to finish off the rhyme
I've done the final test
I admit that perhaps it's true
We are the very best!

(Are her toes crossed as well?
Pity - You can never tell!)

Be ye man or be ye wimmin
Be ye cumin' or be ye gwine
Be ye early or be ye late
Don't forget to shut the gate!

Judith
***

I 'm sending my best wishes
For Christmas cheer
I hope you'll enjoy
The season that's ever so near.

I hope you'll receive

All the presents you desire
And unlike children's toys
These presents you'll never tire.

And if you want a present
From good old, St. Nick
He'll have to be cleverer than clever
And not miss a trick.

On Christmas Eve
He'll not locate Judith's chimney
So under her mat
She'll have to leave him a key.

But there awaits a special treat
Mince pies, sherry and plenty of sweets
But he'll have to leave
By window and tied linen sheets.

(That's in order to avoid a certain squeak
On the door to her house
So no-one is left stirring
Not even a mouse...)

So if I see a man
Climbing outside your wall
I'll know where he's been
And the police I'll not call.

He'll have a jolly white beard
With a baggy red suit

Still holding his sack of presents
Like a burglars loot.

And when I see you next
I'll not say a thing
Although I might ask -
What - *please tell* - did Santa bring?

Merry Christmas!

John
***

*W*hen you have a moment
Would you give my door a knock?
Santa couldn't find your stocking
No pillowcase - no sock.

He surely had a problem
Where could he leave his wares?
Ah, he thought - someone I know
Will lump them down the stairs.

So cluttering up my little flat
There's something in a bag
It must be yours, at least your name
Is written on the tag.

I thank you for the clever rhyme
Note the worthy praise!
I'll try to keep the present mood
For six (or seven) days.

But now I have some chores to do
My flat's a sorry sight
But you will get your poem
When I have time to write.

Thank you for the Christmas card
Now I'm somewhat stressed
Like Santa I've a problem
Just who's the very best?!!

It is the festive season

So there won't be any test
I'll refrain - but only this once
To name the very best

Judith
***

*T*hanks for the good wishes
Returned in good measure
Have a nice Christmas
With plenty of leisure.

Maybe dear Santa
Will call at my flat
I don't think I'd better
Leave the key under the mat.

But I simply must see him
Just think what I'd lack
Sweeties - mince pies
All good things in his sack.

We both have a problem
Abundantly clear
He needs a good chimney
There isn't one here.

With my super brain
A solution I've found
I'll wait up and catch him

(Not making a sound).

Ignoring the squeak
But I think of that sack
The interesting bundle
He has on his back.

When it's time to say goodbye
A little plan I know
If Santas's not too tipsy
(Where did my whisky go?)

I'll lend him sheets and tell him
Try hard not to fall
I'll watch him (and his empty sack)
Abseiling down the wall!

It is the festive season
So there won't be any test
I'll refrain - but only this once
To name the very best.

Judith
***

I hope you had a visit
From good, old St. Nick
And if he didn't make a sound
He didn't miss a trick.

And you must have been nice
For him to come and visit
Naughty means - no presents
I think that's implicit.

But this isn't about Santa
And reindeer that sprout flying wings
It is to thank you profusely
For some of my favourite things.

The presents were lovely
I've really wanted to say,
Opening them up on Christmas Eve
Really made my Christmas Day.

The day planner was splendid
It will really help me to see
My whereabouts each day
And where I should really be.

The book was a treat
This gift you gave to me
I'll soon be an expert
On Devon Heritage and History.

The chocolates as ever
Are a treat indeed
You are intuitive about my mind
You seem to easily read.

Tucked in that "doggy" bag
Was a bottle of the best
And saving it for a rainy day
Will really be quite a test.

Now it's nearly all over

For another year
It's time to take stock
With the decks still to clear.

Are your quarters like mine?
In dreadful disarray,
I've a feeling this will be repeated
Just the same on New Year's Day.

Are your shelves and pantry bare?
All the sherry has been drunk
And the day before yesterday
The last glass has been sunk.

Tiny crumbs of Christmas Pud
And left-over turkey?
Put it in a casserole pot
The result we'll wait and see.

Bows and wrapping paper
Still lay in a mess
The cleaning and tidying up
Is still something to address.

But I hope it was all worth it
And you had a pleasant time
I thought I would ask you
In my last '2006' rhyme.

Because you deserve it

You are one of a kind
And you're a pretty great poet
With each verse easily rhymed.

So to the Brilliant Mind -
The Bard sends good cheer
With hopes that we will continue
Writing our banter for another year.

So my final words for this,
A toast and glass tipped to you
That we'll rhyme articulately in '07
Just as we always (and wittily) do!

John
***

*T*hank you for the poem
  Yes - Santa filled my sack
  One thing I really wish
He'd take his wrappings back.

Now I have to tidy things
And get all spick and span
Not that I'm fond of sweeping up
But I must prove that I can.

I may go walking about
As though I'm in a trance
But naughty - oh - regrettably no
I never get the chance!

I'm glad you liked the doggy bag
Were you sorely pressed?
Not to swig the contents
Of that bottle of the best.

A nasty cough you seem to have
Just take a shot of whisky
Guaranteed to kill all bugs
(And leave you very frisky!)

Too frisky perhaps to man your post
And work is not too pressing
Have the day off just to prove
Your cold turned out a blessing!

Best - That little word reminds me

That I should mend my ways
And never ridicule your rhymes
At least for 5 more days!

Mind you use that planner
That's what you have it for
And what will be on the notice board
"On Duty" - that's for sure.

Now I must end this poem
Not with usual jest
For New Year I will wish you,
All the very best!

(How's that!)
Judith
***

Now you're hearing music
Disturbing your tranquil night
It's just a few notes here and there
Although that doesn't make it right.

It seems it is a mystery
And what is its source?
If it's coming through the ceiling
It really must be full-force.

It may be a xylophone playing
An announcement by way of a tune

Saying dinner is served
It'll be on the table very soon.

Now it's a problem door
To be painted in glossy white
Be sure you've tidied up (and put your clothes on)
Or passers-by will have quite a sight!

These things are sent to try us
Don't let it get you down
Painted doors and xylophones
Are not worthy of a frown.

It's all quite trivial
The painting will only take a week,
Remember you're already fortified
From dealing with last year's squeak.

It's not so much annoying
It's a musical answer you require
Not knowing from where it's coming
Has really got your ire.

I will investigate;
This music that you've heard
If you're sure it's not one too many whisky's
I'll have a quiet word.

I'll knock upon their door
And ask a question or two
Peer around the door

And ask, 'is that xylophone new?'

Perhaps it was from Santa
A gift to them instead of you
He couldn't climb the stairs to yours
And left it in situ.

But I'll ask very casually,
'Do they play it very often?'
And if they do,
'Please could they make the C sharp soften?'

I hope that will help
To put you on an even keel
So your temper is not spinning off
Like a rogue (or fifth) wheel.

Because I hope that living at Raleigh
When all said and done,
Is nearer Heaven than Hell
And not miserable but fun!

John
***

*A*propos the music?
3 notes at the most
What it is, I know not
Must be Santa's ghost.

Maybe in his kindness
He'll visit me quite soon
And bring me some more whisky
And I won't hear that tune.

The door indeed was painted
By a man whose name was also John
He kept the door discreetly closed
Until my clothes were on!

Raleigh Court near Heaven?
But Heaven can be hell
If all you hear from down below
Is noise you cannot quell!

But there I expect they do enjoy
Trying to play the harp,
But I do wish they'd change the key

Say something like C sharp?

My temper now has simmered down
The men are still around
Through all that slapping on of paint
They rarely make a sound.

Now I'll take the rubbish down
But has that damn door stuck?
I wouldn't be surprised you know
Just my rotten luck!

Recall the ancient saying;
'The straw fell out the sack'
The very last one - but it proved
To break the camel's back.

Break my back it will not
My woes are off my chest
Now I'll try to keep to that
At least I'll do my best.

Judith
***

As the saying goes,
'Rome wasn't built in a day',
And Raleigh won't be painted till next week
Or so they say.

But let's hope the music maestro
Will quit quite soon
And you can give up playing,
'Name that Tune'.

But first things first
Your door looks spick and span
That lick of paint
Makes it look the best that it can.

But do you have the urge
To get your paint brush out?
Paint your door purple
And the rules we will flout.

On second thoughts
That may not be so clever
The neighbours might copy us
Although never say never.

I'll find a host of coloured doors
Purple, green, cherry red and aqua blue,
And I shouldn't wonder
A few other colours too.

So I'll stick to plain, old white

And conform just like the rest
And tear up my
Colour-coded request.

It's a funny thing isn't it;
When a sign says, "paint is wet"
We'll eye it suspiciously
Until disbelief and confirmation is met.

Curious fingers
Will touch that sticky paint
To resist doing this,
Takes the action of a saint.

We'll discover, "Wet" didn't mean "Dry"
And now that we know
Guiltily we'll creep off
Quietly by tippy-toe.

So if sticking your fingers in paint
"Floats your boat"
Relax – remember,
It's still just the undercoat!

John

*M*usical Maestro??!! I note Fred
Decided to make his day
Saturday evening - a good time
To have his little play!

Can't say I was very thrilled
He wouldn't get my vote
I've tried and tried but cannot make
A tune from just one note.

Regarding door - I've done my best
There's not one finger mark
But I've a mind to paint it red
My goodness — "*wot*" a lark!!

All the folk would stop and stare
And wonder at the sight
But it would make a welcome change
From boring, dreary white.

Now it's Monday morn again
And you must face your day
I send this little poem
To help you on your way.

Did you have a good weekend?
Nothing happened here
Only our lone chanter
And he was in top gear!

How sad it was on Friday

My spirits promptly dived
No cheerful face at office door
I really felt deprived.

But there - come Monday morning
We shall see your smiling face
As to previous sadness
Happily not a trace!

(I have been debating
Who is the greatest pest?
I've come to the conclusion
Our 1-note Fred is best!)

Judith
***

Perched high on St. Swithens Hill
In my new nest
I had a fleeting thought;
Is Judith still the best?

Inspired by dazzling vistas
Of Dartmoor,
Has brought my rhyming ways
Right back to the fore. (I can hear your sigh from here!)

Looking back at my time
At the Court of Raleigh,
I do affectionately recall
Receiving your lovely poems each day.

The Bard misses the wit
Of the Brilliant mind
Poets here of your Calibre
Are not easy to find.

Historically delivered
By my fair hand,
This poem comes to you
By way of the Royal postman.

I'll hope for a visit sometime
From your good self
To the Bard's new abode
And we'll drink to good health.

I'm at number 45
Montgomery Court,
Stop by for drinks
Or if you're simply caught short.

I've made 2 copies
Of all the poems we've penned,
One for my coffee table
One for my dear friend.

At an appointed cafe
I'll give your copy and keepsake
We can recite our old writings
Over hot coffee and cake.

Until that time we meet again
I hope this ditty will do
I'll keep writing
In hopes that you do too.

The Bard will sign off
With his usual flair
And challenge the Brilliant Mind
To match his lofty air!

P.S. That wasn't a dog on that card
It's the size of a horse
It would tower above Lahti
But she'd still chase him of course.

John

Y*ou might live right at the top
But here's what I suggest
Let's get it straight before we start*
One only can be best.

*Having sorted that one out
The maestro will begin
And if my poems cause you stress
Just take it on the chin.*

*Your rhyming days are to the fore
At least that's what you've written
It could be wishful thinking
Or that green-eyed bug has bitten!*

*What mischief are you hatching
With my super-clever verse?
I smell a rat - a big one too,
In fact a skunk - that's worse!*

*Expect I'll calm down
In the fullness of time
And I'll know the fate
Of those poems of mine.*

*Away with the prose
I'm off for a ride
Did I say a trip?
More like a slide!*

The drive is a hazard

Wet leaves everywhere
And no one about to
Say, 'morning - take care.'

But I'm not down-hearted
I just live in hope
No "A" over "H"
As I go down the slope.

(Up or down - left or right
It wouldn't be a pretty sight).

Cafe's and coffee
Will always please me
Especially if all of
The goodies are free.

I've read through your effort
No comment to pass
I'm thankful I've come to the ending -
At last!

I think I'd better take that back
In case it seems unkind
I won't forget the apple cart
Cake and coffee on my mind!

Lahti chase that gorgeous dog
That would be a lark
On the sofa she would leap
She wouldn't even bark!

Have I lost my skill at verse?
My talent been repressed?
Ask a silly question
Of course I'm still the best!

Judith
***

Your prose repressed? You wanted to know,
 If not exactly rust-free
 It's been a few weeks
Practice is surely the key.

But stifle that frown
You'll soon be in the groove
Writing fresh poetry
That should illuminate and move.

Carry on reading
You'll soon get the gist
Of how to write prose
That's truly sun-kissed!

You say there's only room for one
To be the very best
I think you say that
In an attempt to joke or maybe jest.

That sparkling and witty verse

You so desire to write
Can be nearly as elusive
As flying a kite.

No strings attached
Excessive wind unnecessary
It's down to imagination
And one's own ability.

But like that kite
I must reluctantly say,
Your take-off and landing does create
Quite a melee.

And if you should let go
Of that tightening string
The queen of prose will be lost
And I'll be the king!

And if your crown is gone
Like that kite in the sky
And instead of the best
You'll be served humble pie.

And when you come down
From the clouds up there
And get back to earth
The title we might share.

All that talk of rats and skunks
Have you in retreat

No-one's going to pull the proverbial rug
From under your feet.

What was the third creature?
I think t'was a bug
Something about envy?
I reply by way of a shrug.

Whatever your comeback
I'm sure it will be sharp
I'll hold my tongue
And I'll not whine or not carp.

As you say in your latest,
I'll take it all on the chin
Better than on the nose
Or a kick in the shin.

Can you match my prose?
I'll be here on the hill
Waiting for your rhyming reply
It could be a month or more still.

And when you do aim for the sky
With prose - like that flying kite
Remember to steer and direct
And to hang on ever-so tight!

John
***

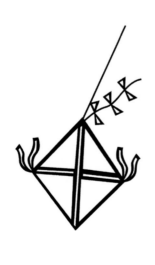

*R*eally - living at the top
Has gone right to your head
Pride always goes before a fall
That's what the experts said.

Apparently you live in hope
That you might be king
Ever optimistic - but
Your rival has a sting.

Expertly I fly my kite
The string is never slack
Wound around my finger tight
I'll never lose the knack.

You think I'd share a title?
Never let it be thought
Alone I am queen
And I'll keep that string taut!

Glad you've got the sense
To take my comments on the chin
There could have been a battle
Now I wonder who would win.

Of course I know who that would be
Needs no explanation
I would watch the loser go
Towards annihilation!!

There was a mention once of cake
My hopes they surely rose
But hope deferred - the heart is sick
That's as the saying goes.

I've plodded through your poems
I suppose I was impressed
But I must make it clear
That I am quite the very best.

Sometimes I sit and ponder
Do you ever spare a thought
For all your ex-admirers
Who live at Raleigh Court?

Judith
***

I sit here feeling very sad
All is gloomy - all is bad
All is cloudy - nothing bright
Another boring day in sight.

A fight to move - the spirits weak
I'm much afraid, the outlook's bleak
Damn - there goes the wretched phone
Careful now - I mustn't moan.

Who can it be, to mar my thoughts?
(I guess I'm feeling out of sorts!)

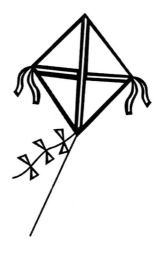

But now I feel a different girl
No longer sad but all awhirl.

My trusty friend a greeting sent
My dismal thoughts a' flying went!

Judith
***

I was glad to help
It was really overdue
A simple phone call
To halt your rhapsody in blue.

Your dismal thoughts
After six or seven rings
Did take speedy flight
Like a bird with flapping wings.

That mood of gloom
And melancholy voice
Now has swiftly gone
Is reason to rejoice.

Now it is vanquished
What shall we do?
T'is an effort to find
Topics anew.

I could continue my banter
But with your recent disposition
I really should be sensitive
And do nothing but listen.

I will tell you my good news
About my recent week
No sight of leaking water
Or the sounds of a squeak…

It may not seem exciting

To have such a peaceful time
But when all about me is quiet
Then I can write this little rhyme.

These things are very pleasing
As you are well aware
When all is so quiet
I really don't have a care.

But calm or busy alike,
Before the day's been and gone
I'll take one final look up;
To check the roof is still on!

John
***

The other day I found there was
A letter on the mat
With invitation <u>and</u> a verse
(How did you manage that?).

I had no worries - all was well
The atmosphere was calm
But visions of some would-be poem
Just filled me with alarm.

But now I've read your little verse
I must say I'm impressed

But don't get too excited
Remember I'm the best!

I'll ring off now - a job to do
(I'm not entirely willing)
I have to clean my little flat
Alas - not very thrilling.

Az you zay - zee you!

Judith
***

I have recently been sent
To a course for First Aid
Refreshing my skills
Presumably, I still got paid?!

Resuscitation and triangular bandaging
Were all the rage
Practicing these was the reason
To allow me out of my "cage".

Now I am back
Nothing much is new
Although if someone wants
I'll bandage them up on cue.

Should they be bleeding
Say, just a small cut
I'll be there with dressing
Saying, 'there, there' and 'tut-tut-tut'.

Even with my new certificate
For CPR and the rest
I hope there's a lengthy time
Before my very next "real" test.

So with great reluctance
To try out these "refreshed" skills
I'll remind one and all
to keep taking their prescribed pills!

And I hope and pray
The only required therapy from me
Is one that is soothed by
Sympathy and cups of tea.

But if duty calls,
I'll bandage them from head to foot
Just like that famous Egyptian
The mummified boy king, "Toot". (Tut)

If it is more serious
Say, in the nature of an antidote
I'll be hastily calling 999
And grabbing their hat and their coat.

So when you come to visit

And you see my First Aid kit,
Please be ever-so patient
I'm just off to do my "bit".

If indeed - it's something trivial
And there's no need for a quack
I'll go about my work
And do the famous "*Kemp-Bard*" wrap!

John
***

*W*as in the garden yesterday
Received a nasty sting
How did that occur you ask?
Well - could be anything.

But I can't find a medic
Although I've looked around
I've come to the conclusion
They're quite thin on the ground!

I know someone who might have helped
(Just a fleeting thought)
But he is miles and miles away
No longer at the Court.

A shame because he seems so keen
To do his First Aid bit
Bandaging - massaging - oh dear me
Where's the end to it?

It seems I'll have to keep my sting
I cannot get it dressed
But badly wounded though I am
At least I'm still the best!

Judith
***

I've just received a magazine
Of carefully written verse

Dutifully I've read it
(It goes from bad to worse)

Those poems - who composed them
Whoever could it be?
As half of them are brilliant
I think it must be me!

(Dreadful grammar - such a crime -
But I had to make it rhyme)

Which half?
Why ask!

Then some author sent a book
I had to read it - know the bloke
Must have sent me off to sleep
T'was almost midnight when I woke.

Now stop - I've just remembered
I shouldn't cause you pain
As you supplied the coffee
I'll start the book again.

Now I'm halfway through
I've got to have a little break
Some jobs need frequent sustenance
Like coffee and cake!

I've done my shopping - cleaned the flat
Now for light relief

Nothing like a little rest
That is my belief.

A coffee (hot) - a clever book
Would have been the ticket
Alas, the only book I had
Was nothing else but Cricket!

Googly's - Overs - Yorkers - Byes -
Legs - (well of a kind ...)
My head is going round and round
Sure I must unwind...

Off to Library I will go
Lots of books to see
If I'm lucky I might find
A book that's Cricket-free.

I'd better keep the other book
Although I don't play Cricket
As if I did I'd sure to get into
A very Sticky Wicket!

Judith
***

I have been struggling to write
A rhyming verse
I'm starting to think
It must be a curse.

No sound have you heard
Of your favourite muse
No titbits at all
Of my latest news.

You must be wondering
What has broken that curse?
I've re-read all your poems
I've realized - I could hardly do worse!

The days fly by,
Winter into spring
The brilliant mind is silent
Does that make me king?

I'll try to stir you
Out of your lethargy
With a few barbed comments
Sit back, I'll wait and see.

I've looked in the café's
All your favourite haunts
Judith must be off
On one of her jaunts.

Salcombe maybe?
Out for a spin
Or at home - feet up, drinking coffee
And staying "in".

Are you digging in the garden?
With shovel in hand
Enjoying the April sunshine
Looking all tanned.

I'll give you a call
To see what is up
I'll get the biscuits in
And wash your favourite cup.

So what do you think?
Of an invite for a drink
If you can tear yourself
Away from the kitchen sink.

So put down your rusty hoe
Your shovel and your spade
If you come and visit
The coffee's pre-made.

So postpone your trip
To the windy promenade
To forgo this
Shouldn't be too hard.

In a funny, old way
Your "poetry" has inspired me
Re-reading it again
Was surely the key.

So please write me another "verse"
You can patently see
The Bard's back on form
I'm sure you'll agree!

(If that doesn't raise your hackles
Nothing will
But my humble apologies
If I sounded too shrill…)

John

*A*lthough I'm rather busy
I'll spare a little time
It won't take me a minute
To write a simple rhyme.

I know some folk take ages
Fifty days or more
Not surprising really
When ability is poor.

But I may have to change my mind
I have a script to read
Glancing through it quickly
I thought - not bad indeed.

Perhaps somebody can write verse
Live and learn we do!
Reading all from tip to toe
Perhaps I'll have a clue.

But first things first - most crucial
Cup and saucer on the table?
(Nicely washed and set just so)
Are biscuits available?

Because I'm really shattered
Done nothing else but dig
Woe is me - my joints are stiff
The gardens far too big.

I had to go to Salcombe

To shrug off all that pain
I'm glad to say it worked - so
I may go there again!

Now I'm feeling better
Not quite the thing I fear
But two digestives and a drink
And I'll be in top gear.

But perhaps I'd better warn you
There's something I must tell
Having had my eyes adjusted
I now can see quite well.

So if the proffered biscuits
Are not the proper make
I'll give them all to Lahti
And settle for some cake!

Judith
*****

"*When I went to hospital*"

I saw a nurse and got some drops
Another nurse - but plus a squirt
Then more drops - perhaps the last?
But at least they didn't hurt.

Directed to another room
I thought that at this rate
I'll never get my poor eye done
I hope it's worth the wait.

Suddenly my name was called
And from where I sat
I saw a man in bright blue pants
And a very peculiar hat!

He said; 'please follow me my dear'
Oh - here we go again
What will happen this time round?
I trust it's not in vain.

I duly followed the funny hat
Into the theatre it led,
Where someone said - don't mind the shoes
Just get yourself on the bed.

I heard somebody mention
This table needs a wedge
Next thing I remember
I tumbled off the edge!

The surgeon - impatient -
Gave a great roar
I can't do her eye
If she's down on the floor.

They levered me up
Put me back on the bed
Ignore the bad eye
See the bump on my head!

After all the kerfuffle
My eye was made good
Still couldn't see much
Because of the hood.

I could just see that man
With the very odd hat;
Turns out he's the surgeon
Well, well - fancy that!

Now all is over
I'm back at the flat
I've forgotten the eye
But remember that hat!

Judith

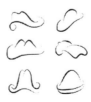

What's been going on there?
Slipping off beds
Upsetting the chief medic
And bumping heads?

Whatever next? Do tell;
Were you fleeing the ward?
Made to return
Forcibly or of your own free accord?

Although that surgeon was quite smart
Your sole memories of the big op.
Seems were limited to
What he wore on top.

So you might say
He really was quite astute
Wearing that funny hat
That was just peculiar rather than cute.

I'm glad it all worked out
Now you've got 20-20 vision
Even though the surgeon's attire
Was the subject of your derision.

The proof is in the pudding
When all is said and done,
I'm happy you're all fixed up now
Tomorrow is a new day begun.

With your like-new eye
And much clearer sight
You can edit
And re-read what you write.

I suppose it was wishful thinking
At the very same time
That surgeon might have helped you
Improve your ability to rhyme.

And your cerebral qualities
That's a whole other matter
Whether they be lesser or greater
(The *former* not the latter).

It'll take quite a doctor to fix it
The best in this southern land
There's still no guarantee
He won't need a helping hand.

Thankfully, your poem explains quite a lot
That recent bump to your head
The results of which
Are best left unsaid.

Most important - I hope you've set a date
For an appointment anew
Another bump to your head
That'll need urgent attention too!

John

First thing I must tell you
The alleged bump on my head
Has not affected brain power
That really must be said.

But what could dim the genius?
Nothing could do that
And my surgeon was most helpful
Never mind the curious hat.

What - me - turned yellow
What made you think I might?
I tumbled off the bed because
The screws were not made tight.

Not because I had cold feet
And tried to chicken out
No - I knew the eye came first
Of that there was no doubt.

Now I can see most clearly
And if by chance I spy
The ex-manager coming up the slope
I can merely close my eye!

Judith
***

Finale:

*W*e've had some good laughs and had some fun
     Now for the final score,
     We both agree the end result -
Has got to be a draw.

Judith
***

Generous you are
     When all is said and done,
     And fair's fair
That neither one of us has won.

John
***

The End

The Barbers Visit

By John Kemp

Off I stroll to my barber
In hopes of a brand new look
From a glossy styling magazine
Or a "coiffure" book.

A doorbell jangles, a hand gestures
For me to take the leather seat
Being treated like a king
Is really quite a pleasant treat.

Like a napkin tucked around my neck
His unfurled cloth covers me
From my chin
To just below the knee.

As if an operation
For my uncovered head
Entrapped there now
Suddenly, I feel nervous and full of dread.

He asks me; 'How have I been?'
I return the courtesy -
(Addressed directly to the mirror)
To avoid moving even one degree.

Because he's now poised with scissors
And a comb gripped in hand
Studying my neglected hair
And pulling on a noodle-size strand!

He tells me, he's been so busy

But insists, he's 'doing fine'
Busily cutting hair, shampooing
And adding conditioner to shine.

Then a sigh and mock gloom
He's looking outside as if in vain
In hopes of cheery sunshine
Instead of constant rain.

I look beyond my dangling feet
To his stock on the far wall
Curling tongs, gels and lacquers
All things to help one walk tall.

Expectantly he awaits,
For instructions by my request
Of what to do
To *this* lofty "feathered" nest.

But in that mirror
I witness my barber's frown
And pretend not to notice
His dismissal of my fair crown.

A spray of water
His comb ruffles through my mane
I soon realize what his expression means;
It's "search and rescue" time again.

That my head is follicle-challenged
Has left me still and shaken

I look back once again
In hopes he may be mistaken.

He speedily sets off to work
On creating a brand new hair-do
In next to no time
He's finished trimming my sideboards too.

He brushes away those scratchy hairs
A spray of gentleman's "perfume"
He says with finality;
'All is done for your new plume!'

I give hearty thanks
And he gives me the bill
I've got two five pound notes
Specifically tucked in my pocket still.

As I catch my reflection
I do a preliminary count;
Of those fast disappearing hairs - and contemplate
How the charge is *always* the same amount!

Still, I'll make an appointment anew
Until that time, my hair no longer needs a trim
I'm glad to say,
I'm not yet bald - just gray and going thin.

So I'll be on my way
With a whistle and a carefree shrug
It could be much worse;

I could be in need of the "comb-over" or even a rug!

***

The Dentist

By John Kemp

I gingerly sit in the dentist's chair
Laying right back
I imagine what torture might be like
On an authentic medieval rack.

My cowardice precedes me
For it is a shocking sight
Seeing his "bag of tricks" again
Give me thoughts of taking flight.

I liken my dentist to a car mechanic
Fixing an old engine
But, of course working on me
Not on an old piece of tin.

He leans forward
And rolls those big eyes
I feel slightly perturbed
At his towering size.

Something comes over him
A smile - no - a smirk,
His fingers loitering over his instruments
All impatient to start work.

I wince and I cringe
In readiness for mind-numbing pain
I make a private vow
Never to visit him again.

Then he begins to
Smile and chatter away
As if to put me at ease
My fears to allay.

He tells me to holler
If I should feel pain
There's no need for him to worry
I'll shriek with no shame.

My mouth he ogles
My view is of his nose
The drill whirrs on my gum
Suddenly, I can't feel my own toes!

'Have a nice weekend?'
A question - more token
I nod a manic affirmative
My mouth a mile wide-open.

With a drill in one's mouth
It's hard to converse
So, I spluttered and babbled
It went from bad to much worse.

'How's your spouse?'

'F-i-n-e' I attempt to say
And he studies my mouth
As if he's discovered major tooth decay.

He stopped still for a moment;
'Do you still floss?'
Naturally, I lie (he has a drill in his hand ...)
I shouldn't wish to make him unhappy or cross!

'Open wider,' he politely requested
What does he expect?
If my mouth opens any bigger
It'll be the next Chunnel-elect.

I strain my jaw muscles
His request I aim to comply
Looking up again
I witness his semi-smile and a sigh.

I try to relax but
My hands grip the chair
Any more pain
I don't think I can bear.

He says; 'think of something nice...'
I imagine flying a kite
Sadly, it crash lands
When a needle comes into sight.

'This shouldn't hurt,'
I gravely nod my head

And wonder if in fact
It would be preferable to be dead.

In hindsight, I have to contradict
My dentist's own view
Because, my dear reader
I cried out on cue.

In fact, I jumped up
Like a man alive from his grave
Not looking back and leaving
Without even a goodbye or a wave.

I was like an Olympic athlete
Sprinting around on a track
For fear of more
Of that sadistic dental-attack.

My dentist simply looked on
As I made my concerns explicit
The receptionist called out;
'Here's a reminder for your next visit...'

The dentist gave out a loud roar
As I escaped right out of the front door.

Though, I heard him clearly say;
'Progress at last! I got him to sit in the chair today!'

Other Books by John Kemp:

Pool of Deceit
ISBN: 9781908147981

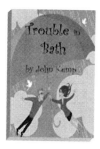

Trouble in Bath
ISBN: 9781907986260

A Sticky Wicket
ISBN: 0918736781

For a sneak peek inside the books, check out the titles
on Amazon.com.

Other purchases (please quote the above ISBN
numbers) can be made at your local Waterstones and
all good book stores.

Coming in 2012 Ten Strands by John Kemp

Thank you to my Publisher Edward Smith and the You Write On team.

.

Lightning Source UK Ltd.
Milton Keynes UK
178440UK00001B/31/P

Cross S/Words

A Duel in Verse

By Judith Putt & John Kemp

Published by YouWriteOn.com, 2011